piano • vocal • guitar

DEMI LOVATO DON'T FORGET

Y0-CAY-463

ISBN 978-1-4234-6664-2

SEVEN PEAKS MUSIC

DISTRIBUTED BY

HAL•LEONARD®
CORPORATION
7777 W. BLUEMOUND RD. P.O. BOX 13819 MILWAUKEE, WI 53213

In Australia Contact:
Hal Leonard Australia Pty. Ltd.
4 Lentara Court
Cheltenham, Victoria, 3192 Australia
Email: ausadmin@halleonard.com.au

Visit Hal Leonard Online at
www.halleonard.com

LA LA LAND

Words and Music by DEMI LOVATO,
NICHOLAS JONAS, JOSEPH JONAS
and KEVIN JONAS II

(1., 2.) *Guitar solo ad lib.*

Well, some may say I need ___ to be a - fraid ___

___ of los - ing ev - 'ry - thing ___ be -

(La,   la,   la,

la,   la,   la.)

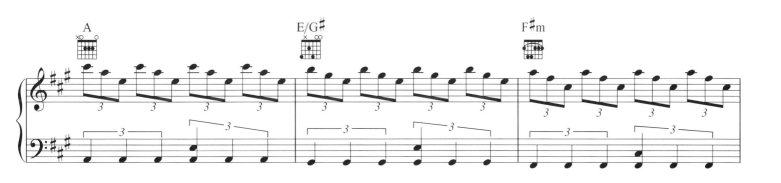

GET BACK

Words and Music by DEMI LOVATO,
NICHOLAS JONAS, JOSEPH JONAS
and KEVIN JONAS II

TRAINWRECK

Words and Music by
DEMI LOVATO

* Recorded a half step higher.

PARTY

Words and Music by DEMI LOVATO,
ROBERT SCHWARTZMAN and JOHN FIELDS

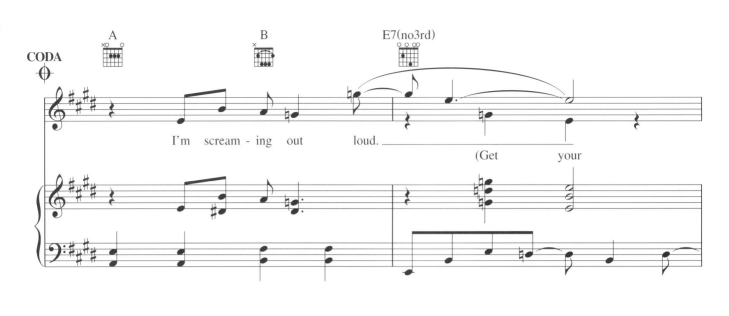

I'm scream - ing out loud. _____ (Get your

par - ty on, ___ get your, get your par - ty on.) __
(Lead vocal ad lib. to end)

(Get your par - ty on, ___ get your, get your

par - ty on.) __   *Spoken: Let's do it again!*

ON THE LINE

Words and Music by DEMI LOVATO,
NICHOLAS JONAS, JOSEPH JONAS
and KEVIN JONAS II

44

DON'T FORGET

Words and Music by DEMI LOVATO,
NICHOLAS JONAS, JOSEPH JONAS
and KEVIN JONAS II

GONNA GET CAUGHT

Words and Music by DEMI LOVATO,
NICHOLAS JONAS, JOSEPH JONAS
and KEVIN JONAS II

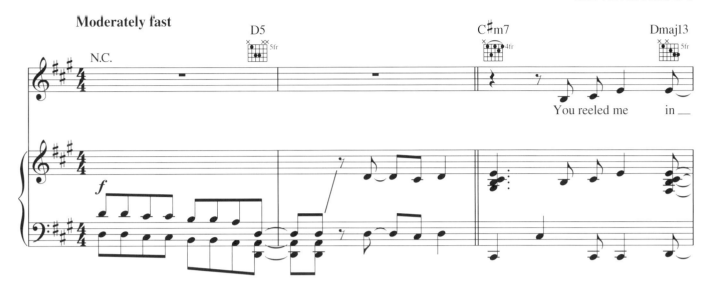

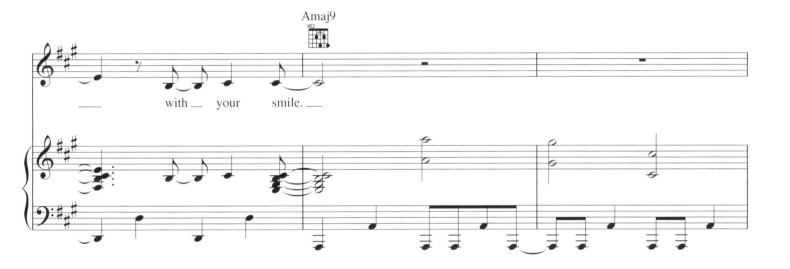

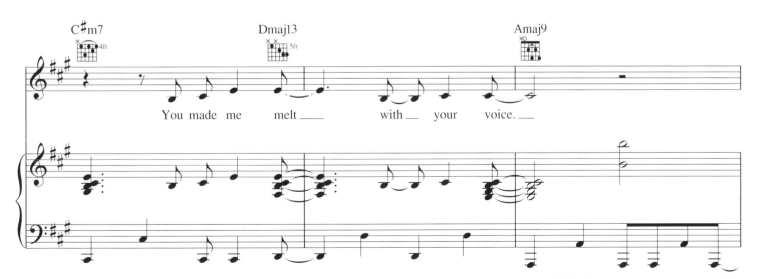

TWO WORLDS COLLIDE

Words and Music by DEMI LOVATO,
NICHOLAS JONAS, JOSEPH JONAS
and KEVIN JONAS II

THE MIDDLE

Words and Music by JASON REEVES,
KARA DioGUARDI and JOHN FIELDS

UNTIL YOU'RE MINE

Words and Music by ANDY DODD
and ADAM WATTS

*Recorded a half step lower.

BELIEVE IN ME

Words and Music by DEMI LOVATO,
KARA DioGUARDI and JOHN FIELDS

Moderately

Lyrics:
I'm los-ing my-self, try-ing to com-pete with ev-'ry-one else, in-stead of just be-ing me.